Oracles from the Black Pool

ORACLES
from the
BLACK POOL

D. L. Myers

Illustrated by Dan Sauer

Hippocampus Press
———————
New York

Oracles from the Black Pool copyright © 2019 by Hippocampus Press
Works by D. L. Myers copyright © 2019 by D. L. Myers.
"Introduction," "The Dark Road to Harrow," and "Black Oracles"
    copyright © 2019 by K. A. Opperman.
"With a Love So Vile" copyright © 2019 by Ashley Dioses.
"The Silver Gate" copyright © 2019 by Adam Bolivar.

Cover artwork and interior illustrations copyright © 2019 Dan Sauer.

All rights reserved. No part of this work may be reproduced in any form or by any means without the written permission of the publisher.

Published by Hippocampus Press
P.O. Box 641, New York, NY 10156
www.hippocampuspress.com

Cover artwork and design by Daniel V. Sauer, dansauerdesign.com.
Hippocampus Press logo designed by Anastasia Damianakos.

First Edition
1 3 5 7 9 8 6 4 2

ISBN 978-1-61498-243-2 trade paperback
ISBN 978-1-61498-259-7 ebook

*To Ashley Dioses and Kyle Opperman
for their assistance and unfailing support,
and to Linda, Chelsea and Will who always believed in me.*

Contents

Origins of the Oracle, *by K. A. Opperman* 11
I. The Streets of Yorehaven 15
    Cold Creek Campground 17
    Along Icicle Creek 18
    The Bone Grove 19
    The Streets of Yorehaven 20
    The Dark Road 21
    Harrow 22
    The Black Road 24
    The Palisade 25
    The Tree and the House 28
    Dark House of Hunger 30
    The Well 31
    Beyond the Veil 38
II. The Acolytes of Samhain 41
    Autumn Moon 43
    The Littlest Werewolf 44
    The Demon Corn 46
    The Death of Twilight 48
    The Acolytes of Samhain 49
    On All Hallow's Eve 50
III. The Summons 53
    The Summons 55
    Night Shrikes 57
    Vul Ravin 59
    Black Tomb Flowers 60
    The Dark Spaces of the Trees 61
    Haiku One 62
    Dreamclouds 63
    Haiku Two 64
    An Owl Haunts My Dreams 65
    Death's Head 67
    Nightfall 68
    Incense 71
    The Thing on the Mountain 72
    The Cave of Ebon Boughs 74

The Phosphorescent Fungi 76
Haiku Three 77
The Raven's Lament 78
If All the Seas Were Blood 80
A Memory of Ocean Lost. 81

IV. The Star's Prisoner 83
A Caul of Luminance 85
After the Light 86
The Dark Stars 89
The Star's Prisoner 90
The Stars Are Black 92
At the End of Day 94

V. The Canker Within 95
The Demon Road 97
The Canker Within 98
Terror 100
Jack's a Kidder 102

VI. The Temple of the River Goddess 103
Hazel 105
Haiku Four 106
The Temple of the River Goddess 107
Waterfalls 108
You Are a Temple in a Moonlit Meadow 109
To L—— 110
Transcended Vision 111
Allegory 112
Ashiel's Garden 113
Aisha's Revenge 115

VII. O Dark Muse 117
Kylen-Xyr 119
The Sorcerous Scribe 121
The Crimson Kist 122
Word Painting 123
O Dark Muse 124
Poetry Is Sorcery 126

VIII. Tributes 127
With a Love So Vile 129
The Silver Gate 130
The Dark Road to Harrow 133
Black Oracles 134

Illustrations

Harrow	23
The Palisade	26
Dark House of Hunger	29
The Well	33
Beyond the Veil	39
The Demon Corn	47
On All Hallow's Eve	51
The Summons	56
Vul Ravin	58
An Owl Haunts My Dreams	66
Nightfall	69
The Thing on the Mountain	73
The Phosphorescent Fungi	75
If All the Seas Were Blood	79
After the Light	87
The Star's Prisoner	91
The Canker Within	99
Jack's a Kidder	101
Ashiel's Garden	114
O Dark Muse	125
Black Oracles	135

Origins of the Oracle

I first became acquainted with D. L. Myers through our mutual involvement in the now long-defunct online journal, *The Absent Willow Review*. His poem "Nightfall," dedicated to each of the Big Three of *Weird Tales* (H. P. Lovecraft, Clark Ashton Smith, and Robert E. Howard), was first published in one of its issues, and upon reading it I immediately felt a poetic kinship with its author. I felt the urge to pay him a compliment, and so, having obtained his email from the editor—the author first having provided permission for me to receive it—I wrote to Mr. D. L. Myers expressing my appreciation of his poem. This was to spark a long-running correspondence that would prove very fruitful for both of us, and which would shape the early years of our respective careers. We both began our journeys writing for this magazine, and our literary paths would remain entwined from then on. Mr. Myers remains my longest running literary correspondent; I have known him longer than any other writer.

Though we did not yet know it, my friendship with Mr. Myers was to form the core of what would eventually come to be known as The Crimson Circle—a group of four contemporary Dark Romantic poets with similar aims and subject matter. When Ashley Dioses, and then Adam Bolivar, eventually gravitated into our group—for such was the strong pull of fate—the Circle was completed.

Without a doubt, D. L. Myers remains the most mysterious and reclusive member of The Crimson Circle, but his eremitic tendencies do not correspond with any lack of ability. On the contrary, these poems reveal a practiced hand and a tightness of expression that are the hallmark of formal poetry. But whether in formal verse, free verse, or blank hybrids of the two, D. L. Myers succeeds in weaving a deadly sorcery that poisons the blood, spreading like the black branches of a blighted tree, taking root in the very heart and sucking unspeakable nourishment from the very pits of the soul.

A unique sort of *savageness* pervades these poems, of a sort that I have not encountered anywhere else. In fact, that is the one word that has always come to my mind when I have contemplated D. L. Myers's poetry over the years—*savage*. What I mean by that is *powerful, primal, twisted, malevolent* even, like poison roiling, seething, and hissing in a witch's cauldron. These poems reach from the pages with crooked claws to physically assault the reader, slashing, twisting, breaking bone. The cumulative, concentrated effect of pure darkness that emanates from many of these poems is, quite simply, staggering.

While these poems cover a wide array of subjects, from the purely horrific to the tender and romantic, it is the poetry of Nature—whether of invented locales or of actual shunned corners of the Pacific Northwest—that seems to be D. L. Myers's most beloved province. Written in an unmistakably Lovecraftian vein, but further warped by the black gyre that is the author's imagination, these poems are hymns to the primordial shadow that oozes in the dark spaces between the trees. Nature is seen as a sort of hungry, voracious entity expressed in myriad forms, whose only use for mankind is as pathetic sustenance, his mind but a feeble plaything to be shattered by an awful gnosis. And Mr. Myers is the High Priest of this entity, dwelling in Her benighted temples, singing Her autumnal hymns of decay, death, and ruin. He is the Oracle of the Black Pool, bent over the venomous waters of the woodland tarn, contemplating his own hooded and bearded reflection, seeing only the darkness and the cold, hateful stars that leer down from above the grotesquely branched tree-tops, ghosts in a lightless sky.

Just how D. L. Myers got his moniker The Oracle of the Black Pool I cannot quite recall, though I am almost certain I myself bestowed it on him, inspired by the poisonous pools of Vul Ravin, a vicious, fever-inducing forest of his own invention. Whatever the case, he took on the mantle very early on in our friendship, and it has now affixed itself to him as surely as his own shadow—both the physical phenomenon as well as the night-side of his spirit. Indeed, he has earned the name, scrawling his noxious rhymes and incanting them at various unspeakable festivals with all the power and tremulous sonority of thunder itself.

In everyday life, D. L. Myers is a quiet, mild-mannered man, someone you might foolishly mistake for being somewhat ordinary; but in his poetry, and when possessed by the shadow-persona of the Oracle, a terrific transformation occurs. Poetry, or art in general, can be a medium wherein our shadow selves can express themselves, and in D. L. Myers's case this is ecstatically evident. A sense of benighted liberation haunts this book, even when juxtaposed with surface-level themes of imprisonment and hopelessness, and it may be that the reader will come to know their own shadow better by reading from this tainted hymnal. Open yourself to the darkness, both within and without, and read these tenebrous Oracles From the Black Pool.

—K. A. Opperman

Corona, California
March 2019

I. The Streets of Yorehaven

∽ Places ∽

Cold Creek Campground

In the night that darts and rears like raging
Black adders striking at a beast of flames,
The boy and his father stand in firelight.
They talk of shadows and listen to the
Dark, gruesome tales of Robert E. Howard
While creeping darkness spreads like viscous tar,
And the firelight is all the world they own.

Along Icicle Creek

Along Icicle Creek, the evergreens crouch
And turn their gnarled faces to the shadows
While black and cold waters hiss through the stones
And only dead leaves fill the shallows.

There broken and bare, a long trail leads on
Scant steps from the water's mad dancing,
And it climbs through the mist and the motionless air
To a grove of black trees that are standing

Like dread totems of death with a thousand mad masks
That grimace and stare in the twilight,
While the dark waters flee from their reaching black boughs,
And the foul ground that glimmers with witch light.

And as the night falls, the trail climbs toward the stars
That flicker and flare like hot embers,
And the path is lost then to the infinite sky
With its nightmares and dreams none remembers.

The Bone Grove

There is a beach where shadows stain the rocky ground,
And cairns of coal-black pebbles rise in silent prayer—
To blasted, sun-bleached totems reaching for the sky
Like crucified and tortured men left to decay.

A grove of gouged and naked firs that stand between
A black and brooding wall of trees and swirling fog—
And boundless, raging ocean waves that catapult
Gigantic skeletons upon the stony shore.

Like sacrifices, cold and deathly pale, they stand
Forever bared to wind and sun and starry void,
A testament to all the dark and silent things
That haunt the corridors and dungeons of the soul.

The Streets of Yorehaven

In shifting, swirling veils of acrid mist,
Yorehaven's crouching gambrel roofs lay still
As if a necromancer's spell had kissed
Its darkling streets with his eternal will.
Through maze-like streets and alleys dire and dim,
I wandered under cold and sentient suns
That burned above the crooked paths like grim
And spectral eyes the icy moonlight shuns.

And in the midnight hour, alone and chilled,
My aimless ramble reached its cryptic end
Before a dark and brooding tavern filled
With haunted dreamers' visions that portend
Of fearsome journeys down a nameless road
Where terror harries like a searing goad.

The Dark Road

One moonlit night I found myself alone
Before a dark and brooding, nameless road
That led into a foul and black unknown
Of demon-twisted trees where night abode.
Yorehaven's lozenged windows feebly cast
A sickly glow upon my trembling back
And hissing whispers seemed to speak of vast,
Eternal ill along that evil track.

And then a baleful, chilling wind arose
That pushed me fear-drenched toward that frightful way,
My racing mind aswirl as in the throes
Of some malicious power vile and fey.
Then swallowed by that looming path of doom,
I lost Yorehaven in the misty gloom.

Harrow

In Harrow all the streets head down
To bloated wharves upon a bay,
Of liquid midnight chill and fey,
In which the very moon must drown.

In Harrow shuttered windows cloak
Dim rooms where hissing shadows glide
Like corpses on a starlit tide
Whose fingers brush the waves like smoke.

In Harrow cobwebbed hallways lead
To chambers filled with crumbling scrolls
Of faded glyphs that speak of doles
All lost like chaff from blackened seed.

In Harrow terraced roofs ascend
Into a tattered, cloud-laced sky
Alive with darkling things that fly
Above a silence without end.

In Harrow gelid moonlight clings
To every wall and rooftop vane
And lights the black abysmal fane
To things of dread the twilight brings.

Harrow

I. THE STREETS OF YOREHAVEN

The Black Road

Along the rutted road toward twilight
There is no path of golden light
But only black, eternal spaces,
Soulless voids like starless night,
Where all will find a solemn silence
And dream no more of pain, delight,
Or anything but endless blackness—
A universe of endless night.
So question not the road before you
Or seek to find some grand design;
For there is naught but naught before you
The Black Road and the endless night.

The Palisade

Beyond the grasslands dark, there rises grim
A palisade of mighty logs built high,
Of trees no man remembers or has seen,
To bar all save great vultures soaring nigh.
It was built by Them long forgot and lost
In ages distant and interred in frost.

Though lost to memory, there lingers still
A screaming fear that stains the very soul
Of all that brave that bleak, titanic wall,
And sends them fleeing from their stated goal—
Or else vanished into the mist and fog
Like pebble cast into a weed-choked bog. . . .

The timbers of which the vast wall was built—
Gargantuan logs with crowns sharp like thorns—
Are beyond the ken and reason of man;
Their presence a dark mystery that warns
Of things alien and prehistoric,
Unnamable, vast, phantasmagoric.

The great fence runs unbroken and severe—
Horizon to horizon it extends.
No fine crack or slight gap breaks its expanse,
And impassibility is all it portends;
And the mad, wind-tortured branches of the trees
Shriek like the winds of the lost, distant seas.

The Palisade

What lies beyond that barrier of spikes,
A land of mist-shrouded glacier-bound peaks,
No man has discerned or lived to describe
The silent, frigid heights that no life seeks.
Where the bleak glaciers grind on forever
In the wrack and the wrath of the weather.

Beyond the vast mountains lies the Unknown,
A canvas to be filled with mysteries—
Nightmares and tales of the strange and malign,
And faceless, obscure hidden histories
Of beings and things not safe to reckon,
Lost in the cold with the whispers that beckon.

So the great Palisade has stood and stands,
Immune to the immortal claws of time—
A piece of the world as fixed as the sun
That endures in the soul, dark and sublime,
Like the black forest of fear that laps at the mind,
And where good and evil dwell and are enshrined.

The Tree and the House

There is a row of ancient homes
That line an ancient street,
Where scrawny cats and rabid mice
In silent dance compete.

There standing in a lonely yard
A twisted tree grows foul,
Its bulbous roots plunged in the earth—
Its black leaves like a cowl.

Below its arched and straining limbs
A house lurks like a beast
That waits in breathless, silent pose
For life to join its feast.

For all that cross its threshold fall
To feed its quenchless lust,
And sink through months and years to lie
In cellars filled with dust.

And far beneath the deepest crypt,
The tree's roots pulse like veins
That drink deep of the dark liquor—
The essence that remains.

Dark House of Hunger

Dark House of Hunger

The dark window and dark door appear black
Beneath twisted cedars bent like tortured men
That twitch and dance in the growing dusk.
In a pool of lurking shadow, the shack
Squats and waits like a silent toad,
While glints of light shimmer in the liquid jet
Beyond its window panes and broken door.
Upon the sagging porch, piles of bones erode
Into pale grey dust the wind pushes away.
The breeze whispers balefully in the trees,
While the house, crouching like a vulture, groans
And with rabid hunger awaits its prey.

The Well

1

April 14, 1921

A long and grueling search of many weeks
Had I endured before the house was mine.
The thing that captured me at first a fine,
Old well that stood before its gable peaks.
Of basalt bricks and ebon wood, it stood
Between the house and dark and silent trees
That strangely swayed and shook before the breeze,
As if they yearned to stroke its dusky wood.

I also felt a yearning stir my soul;
A whisper faint and cryptic called to me
Across the endless, shadowed sea of years,
And I may never of its voice be free.
An air of vast and ancient things sublime
About it hung—this thing untouched by time.

2

April 21, 1921

Today, down in the cellar, footing stones
Of countless other structures were revealed,
Each stacked upon the other all concealed,
Beneath a coat of clay inlaid with bones,
Of birds and beasts, arranged into strange signs.
How many there may be, I do not know,
Nor how far under earthen floor they go
Into what lightless depths or hidden mines.

I feel that I am like those stones a part
Of something old and hidden in the earth.
It frightens me and yet allures me too—
This thing unknown that feels about to birth.
What strange, sweet spell sings to me in my sleep?
I fear it calls from someplace dark and deep.

The Well

3

May 30, 1921

My sleep is filled with nightmares foul and black,
Of things half seen or heard in echoes lost,
And I begin to wonder at what cost
To body, soul, and mind these terrors track.
And always I look down into the well
To see a sable, swirling void instead
Of blue and cloudless sky above my head—
Dark dreams of grim foreboding I can't quell.

So, robbed of peaceful sleep, I pass my days
In silent dread of what the night may bring,
What visions strange and vile the wind may sing
In whispers through the trees all lost in haze.
This place begins to feel as if it's cursed;
I fear the dam of doom has yet to burst.

4.

June 19, 1921

This morning in the glowing light of dawn
I found that I had sleepwalked in the night;
I stood before the well aghast and chilled.
A dim-remembered dream filled me with fright—
I saw my face reflected in the well,
A pale and haggard mask of deathly white,
Afloat upon a sea of blinking eyes
That moiled and glimmered in my reeling sight!

Has madness reached into my fevered mind
And left these strange impressions and dark signs—
Or are these things like wind among the pines,
Unseen but sensed in motions all aligned?
I fear that I am lost to savage fate;
For me it is already much too late.

5

July 27, 1921

The voices came in the oppressive heat
Of midnight's gloom, and then I shrank within
My skin too terror-struck by the dire din
To even tremble. Darkness swelled and beat
Its blackness round me like a winding sheet
In which I could not breathe or move or think.
They were a thousand mortal sounds in sync
That swarmed in waves like frenzied bats and beat

Upon my mind a summons fierce and bleak,
Commanding me to climb into the well!
My mind was ever fixed on its black maw;
The voices said there I was meant to dwell.
As dwellers of the past, I would go far
Into the haunted, darkling voids bizarre.

6

August 1, 1921

The former tenants of this place still live,
Below the well's serene, black liquid skin,
Beyond our bright demesne in tracts akin
To ebon gulfs where shapeless things outlive
All life upon this crowded, frantic plane.
Their voices called for me throughout the night,
With darkling words that seared my soul with fright,
To follow them to shadow-worlds arcane.

Today I go to sable spheres unknown,
To realms of being vast and violet-stained
That lie beyond our meager minds constrained
By life within this puny sentient zone.
The well's a door to realms sensed but unseen;
I journey now to where black wings careen.

Beyond the Veil

There is a manor house hoary and grim that stands among vast Chestnut trees that tower like shapeless sentinels about its grey stone walls. Beyond its great, black door, twisting hallways wend in all directions through its nighted interior, where smoking candles provide dim pools of illumination in the crouching darkness. Few have walked these ways, and none have come and gone unchanged by their journey. Those who have spoken of their haunted time within those great, grey walls state that they came in search of an old man who dwells at the heart of the manor. He is said to lie in a great canopied bed whose gauzy shroud extends to all corners of the shadowed ceiling. It stands in the center of an ebony room lit dimly by wall sconces emblazoned with a cryptic sign that glows redly with the waxing and waning of the candles. No accounting of these meetings has ever passed beyond those black paneled walls, yet many have speculated that he speaks words of dark revelation that send these pilgrims onto strange roads with grim tidings. However, one tale has survived. It tells of a girl whose gaze upon entering the black room was drawn upward by the movement of the great pall. In the shifting candlelight, an undulant wave spread toward her across the filmy fabric until its crest stood directly above her. As she stared, the shifting light began to reveal a great cluster of glittering orbs that hovered somewhere beyond the veil. Then with a sudden flare and fading of the crimson light, she realized that what floated between her and the dark ceiling was no canopy but instead an immense web, and the cluster of orbs were the eyes of the weaver.

Beyond the Veil

II. The Acolytes of Samhain

～ Autumn ～

Autumn Moon

The gibbous moon in ruddy cowl
Rides wild in the autumnal sky
While coyotes in the cornstalks howl
And dance to see it soaring high.

The Littlest Werewolf

In a forest of nightmare on a dark mountainside
Lies a black, twisted gorge mist-choked and ice-tortured
Where things of all natures slink, slither, and stalk,
And a pack of werewolves den and shelter.

There the littlest werewolf pounces and howls.
She's the fiercest of beasts in the full moon's bright glow,
Yet down in the village she walks in the sun,
And the villagers know not her secret.

On All Hallow's Eve she walks lone and downcast
Through the streets of the chill, quiet village,
And she wishes to join all the other small ones
On the trail of sweetmeats and confections.

But tonight the full moon will sail brilliant and round
Like a glowing wolf's eye in the heavens,
And the madness will course through her body and blood,
And the wolf will once more gain ascendance.

So she watches the sun sinking into the dusk,
As she wanders off into the forest,
And she shivers with dread and a growing despair,
As the moon rises into the gloaming.

With the madness growing, as the moon climbs the sky,
She lopes off into the moonlit ravine,
And her family of fear takes her into their fold,
And their voices soar hungry and lean.

Soon she reaches the village and stalks through the streets,
Lost in blackness between glowing pumpkins,
And she watches in silence the witches and apes
As they run from one house to another.

Then she chooses her prey, a pale figure of bones,
And begins to move in its direction—
When all at once a strange howl unfamiliar and faint
Comes to her from a dim, crooked alley.

She turns from the bone-boy and creeps toward the sound.
Now an echoing call wild and free:
"Ah—oooh, woo, woo, woo!" comes the sound bright with joy.
It's a werewolf no bigger than she!

In its paws is a sack filled with sweet-smelling treats
That it swings back and forth as it sings,
And she pounces before it and raises her snout
To howl out a greeting loud with glee.

"You're much better than me," the weregirl exclaims.
"Want to get some candy with me?"
And she takes the werewolf's paw and leads her
Through the streets thronged and swirling with fiends.

And the littlest werewolf sheds great tears of joy
As she follows the weregirl into the light,
And the madness recedes and is replaced with a glow
That burns like a jack-o'-lantern's bright smile.

The Demon Corn

All stained with the bloody light of sunset,
The crimson stalks shake and snap in the wind.
The bare field before them glows like a lake of fire,
And on its shore the dead corn dances.
Its rasping voice calls to the ruddy moon
That bulges above the forest cloaked hills,
A sentinel of the endless, black ocean of night.
And as the stars cascade and swirl across the sky,
The stalks wither in shadows
Until they are black and crisp in the night wind.

The Demon Corn

The Death of Twilight

Alone the ruddy leaves in Twilight's grasp
Sail high against the purple sky's dark coat
And paint the rising moon upon the clouds,
A jaundiced eye that foully stares and gloats.

A creeping ground-fog haunts the dying light,
And furtive things peer from within its midst;
Disturbing faces drifting in the brume
With leprous, evil smiles that leer and twist.

All Hallow's Eve has come with Twilight's death,
And witch-light blooms in every pumpkin maw;
Vile glimmers in the inky, spreading night
Where feral demons grope with tooth and claw.

The Acolytes of Samhain

A shrieking, croaking horde, they wheel above the tree—
Their ebon wings unfurled upon the tattered clouds;
An orange moon reflected in their liquid eyes
Like embers sprayed across the twilight sky.

A night-black coven perched amongst the tree's bare limbs,
They glare down glowing eyes aflame with spectral light;
Their heads asway to black devotions, chants, and spells
Arising from the misty earth below.

Cowled figures kneel within a blood-red fairy ring—
A crimson mushroom proffered on each pallid palm—
Oblations rendered to the dusky wings above
That drink their profane words with avid lust.

Dread Samhain's feast has called them all into this night
Where naked witches scream across the star-strewn sky
And half-mad beasts, that once were men, abase their souls
Before things from the black, eternal void.

On All Hallow's Eve

In the swirling treetop's churning
For the autumn sunset's burning
There's a dark and secret yearning
On All Hallow's Eve.

In the orange moonlight's staining,
Of the pallid gravestones' veining,
There are blackened fingers straining
On All Hallow's Eve.

And the icy mists are rising
From the haunted cornstalks prising
At a faded stone's incising
On All Hallow's Eve.

So till midnight watchful keeping
For the things forever creeping
Through the dreams of all the sleeping
On All Hallow's Eve.

On All Hallow's Eve

III. The Summons

⁓ Nature ⁓

The Summons

There is a grim, fog-shrouded forest
Beyond the confines of my room
That whispers of its grottos
And hisses of its dooms.
It calls me with a purpose
That is masked and so obscure—
My mind's aswirl with wonder
At the dark and sweet allure
Of this place of wicked beauty
That seeks some unknown boon
From my mind and trembling body
Beneath the misty winter moon.
And deep within its vastness
I will find a sacred space
Where my wonder will be answered
And my fate I shall embrace.

The Summons

Night Shrikes

Across the dusky sky they swarm and thrash,
Great black hands that beat the cooling air,
Their fingers splayed like fans before the twilight,
Their red eyes burning in the spreading dark.

From the dire forest they burst like an ebon flood
That swirls and arches over rippling grasslands.
A glowing village draws them like grim moths;
Grey fangs and razored talons tear the wind.

A crashing wave, they breach the crystal walls,
Reap with wild hunger the scattering prey within,
Until the only sound is the rending of flesh
And only naked bones greet the silence.

The *Forest of Death* is their mother;
They have suckled at *Her* envenomed breast;
They have arisen from *Her* black maw
To spread *Her* doom beyond *Her* titan verge.

With fierce energy, they lift from stained walls,
A vast, gyring cloud that blots out the stars,
As they return to *Vul Ravin*—to *Her*
The forest of madness and cruel, black death.

Vul Ravin

Vul Ravin

Vul Ravin,
Forest of endings,
Where all light comes to naught
And every path is swarmed by peril.
All things immense, virulent, and fatal
Seek the flame of life on which to feast,
And every organism seeks to savor
The merest glimmer of its illumination.
Lurid blossoms in an opalescent dance of hues
Hide viperous spines whose bite brings
Frenzy, sweat-bright-lunacy, and death,
And the silence is ever fractured by cries
While gyring forms fill the air with slaughter.

A hungry forest of titanic black trees
Teems with quills and talons, spikes and teeth;
Leagues of life insatiable, ever prowling.
Only death finds comfort here,
In quiet pools poisonously colored
And lined with ageless bones,
Upon whose mirrored surfaces
No human eye has stared,
No mortal mind has grasped,
Or realized more than fear.
Vul Ravin,
Forest of terror.
Vul Ravin,
Forest of death.

Black Tomb Flowers

The demons seek the lanthorn blooms
That burn within *Vul Ravin*'s tombs,
Where leprous grey moonlight illumes
The graven faces of the lost and lorn.

There vines surround the walls and domes,
And a baleful beast stalks and roams
Through chiseled passages lined with tomes
By eon-drowned mages that none now mourn.

And with a vile and sickly light
Those blossoms gutter through the night—
Black, viscid things of death and blight
That feed upon the very souls of men.

So, deep within the nether vaults,
Those fiendish flowers sway and waltz,
And all their upas ill exalts
Before crumbling altars beyond all ken.

The Dark Spaces of the Trees

The black interstices between branch and leaf
Crawl with viscous black presences;
Around me the trees are alive with black shapes
That whisper mad riddles and half-glimpsed terrors
While the trees wave in hypnotic rhythms
That seize my mind and drag my soul
Down shadowed corridors that know no end;
The darkness ever growing in the plunge toward nothingness.
Yet the spaces of the trees careen on
Into ever mounting fury.
In the night they press upon me and through me;
I am drawn into their sphere—
See the universes with their eyes.
The wonders and horrors of infinite dimensions
Lie before my naked brain;
Flay my mind with each realization
That I am a blind animal
Cast upon a dust speck,
Insignificant in the totality that is beyond reason.
Then I am back in my yard,
The trees are black blobs against the night,
And all is still and hushed under an electric tension
That holds me captive
Until the trees are lost to sight.

Haiku One

Longing for snowflakes
In hot California sun,
Tree waits for kisses.

Dreamclouds

Psilocin sits,
Watches the silent moment
Pass
Unmindful of the presence.
Clutching the vibrant, green carnation
His fingers softly following
The deep violet valleys.
Eyes reflect slack-velvet-smile
Scan quadrant by quadrant
The shimmering field of visions.
Petals crawl among curled fingerprints
Drop
One by one
To the cold linoleum tile.

Haiku Two

Undulating leaf
Restlessly waiting for wind
To take flight again.

An Owl Haunts My Dreams

It comes in silence spreading wings
Materializing like mist
Above a placid, ebon pool.

Its eyes are pits of molten gold
That fix upon me as I flee
Forever racing toward a wood

Where twisted, lifeless trees surround.
And though I seek to shelter there,
Its burning eyes still pierce me through.

Why It hunts me, I do not know—
Its glare of judgment sears my soul
And fills my days with endless dread.

I fear the coming of the night
And fight the iron bonds of sleep
Where dwells the owl that haunts my dreams.

An Owl Haunts My Dreams

Death's Head

Moth plummets in
Erratic lifting body
On re-entry to endings.
Swings by and dips a wing
Into candle's glare;
Casts a shadow
On wall and retina.
Bone-white semblance on black
Momentarily exposed,
Then folded away into obscurity
Only to return grinning.
Crazy ballerina,
Orbiting extinction,
Your dusky wings
Mark you for eternity.
Pale specter sits;
Waits a lifetime
For you to kiss the light.

Nightfall

for H.P.L., C.A.S., and R.E.H.

The red face of the sun
Leers balefully upon the jagged cliffs
And stains their upthrust faces crimson
With the dying light of day;
While at their feet the shadows moil and pulse,
Like doorways to the black infinitude of space.

And in the final plunge to night,
The blackness crawls upon the scars
To meet the heathered heights above
And drown the vast supernal stars.

What dark, unknown, unguessed regime
Lies beyond our mortal realm
In unseen, infinite voids of being,
Where living darkness burns and swells?

Since long before the fair Valusia—
Before time and even light—
The darkness lived for eons endless
In scintillating waves of spite . . .
Waiting in its insatiable emptiness
For life to step into its maw
To fill the hole that is not fillable,
And suck its living marrow raw.

Nightfall

So now the night hangs on the rock face—
Ebon blackness covers all—
And the earth remains unconscious
Of the silent undertone
That calls from the beginning,
Ever after for all time . . .
The night is falling,
Has fallen,
And will fall forevermore.

Incense

The dragon curls upon the rippling air,
His talons grappling with an unseen foe
That leads him in a swirling, frantic dance
Into the heavens and eternity's close.

The Thing on the Mountain

Across the leagues it stares at me
With yellow-orange eyes of flame
That seek some unknown, ghastly place
Within the tattered thing I call a soul.

With fiendish mirth it scries the doom
That glitters in my haunted eyes
While panic twists my fevered mind
And wraps my form in searing iron chains.

My life is forfeit, ever lost
To glowing cauldrons blazing bright
Upon the mountain's blackened side
Where lurks the lurid thing that claims my life.

The Thing on the Mountain

The Cave of Ebon Boughs

A choking fog obscured my panicked sight,
And all about me blighted shadows danced,
As if infernal harpies soared and pranced
Beyond a churning scrim of mist-fouled night.
And then a parting of the mist revealed
That all around me twisted branches twined
Into a net through which the moonlight shined,
A ghostly glow that in the air congealed.

Then through that cave of ebon boughs
I fled—those horrid shadows pouncing at my heels—
The branches high above me like black eels
That drank the brume and on the moonlight fed,
Until in utter blackness, cold and blind,
I froze in terror body, soul, and mind.

The Phosphorescent Fungi

III. The Summons

The Phosphorescent Fungi

A crawling darkness pressed upon my eyes
In which a moiling sea of phantoms swam,
And crazed, I hungered for a numbing dram
To send my mind to where all reason flies.
Until before me rose a fitful fire,
A corpse-light foul and bruised that chilled my soul
Yet drew me onward toward a ghastly goal—
A grotto burning like a purple pyre!

And then I saw the things that cast that glow,
Pale fungi vile and stained with rank decay;
And bathed in icy sweat from head to toe,
I stood and quaked before that dire display.
Then evil whispers hissed about my ears,
And I broke down in horror wracked with tears.

Haiku Three

Ice-cold, grey rain clouds
Lie broken across blue sky
While I sit gazing.

The Raven's Lament

They say I made the world in my black image
And painted it with feathers drear
To bring all evil into being
And stain the minds of men with fear.
Yet I am but a noble creature,
A thing of flesh and blood and bone,
Who seeks naught but a place in nature
Where beauty fills my soul alone.
So why do all revile and hate me
And flee my visage evermore,
As if I were that bird of darkness
From the night's Plutonian shore?
I will stand this pain no longer;
I will have my just revenge.
And the world will feel my anger,
And my name I will avenge!

If All the Seas Were Blood

If All the Seas Were Blood

If all the seas were blood,
What ships might ply those crimson waves?
What black sands feel their cold embrace?
The sands of a world of basalt and onyx
Pounded by a billion years of bloody breakers
Into bizarre shapes of nightmare.
All is still and filled with the sound of endless, blooming crests
Crashing eternally upon a lifeless world.
A bloated, carmine sun hangs in a claret sky—
The stale air stirs not a grain upon the shore—
Red mists rise from the wine-stained rocks
And ride the wave tops like scarlet dragons.
The weight of eons compresses the very atmosphere,
As if it could press the vital fluid from time itself.
But in this tension there is only emptiness
And the scourging of sanguine waves.

A Memory of Ocean Lost

There was a place unknown, unseen,
Where triremes ranged the foggy shores
And black-winged vultures screamed and keened
While bronze-skinned priests applied their lores.

In ocean vastness lost to time,
Strange wizards plumed the briny depths
That live no more except in rhyme,
A wasteland of a thousand deaths.

Now ghostly sailors rimed with frost
Soar endlessly o'er arid sands
Amongst grey peaks sere, torn and lost
In Time's eternal, taloned hands.

IV. The Star's Prisoner

~ Cosmic Horror ~

A Caul of Luminance

Noctilucent clouds haunt the horizon,
Their glow lambent like ghostly fire—
While the world beneath floats in a caul of brume
That swallows it all like shadows.

After the Light

Mauve clouds in an indigo sky,
Tattered and gauzy like burned-out velvet,
Hover menacingly above vague silhouettes
Of buildings, houses, trees, and hills.
Not a flicker of light breaks the gloom,
Nor hint of movement in the sepulchral darkness.
Night and day are one in the corpse-light
Of the failing taper of a star.
The last night has descended and life has fled,
Like vapor ascending into a black sky.
The faint disc of the moon stands sentinel
Over the mausoleum world,
While the light of living suns form Coronas
Around the dying satellite.
Darkly bruised clouds stream into nothingness,
And then there are only the bright, cold stars,
Red and yellow and blue and piercing white,
Staring down upon the empty streets,
The shriveled orchards, the spine-covered mountains,
The empty fields, the silent gorges where no rivers flow,
And the barren sea stretching
Eternally to the horizon;
Its mountains, valleys, and trenches
Laid bare before the dark heavens;
Its sunken plains littered with whale bones

After the Light

IV. THE STAR'S PRISONER

And the carcasses of wrecked ships.
Then as the guttering candle
Flares and dies, the blackness swallows all
And leaves no trace after the light is gone.

The Dark Stars

Among fiery, astral orbs burning bright
Lurk invisible, sable spheres of Death
That spin eternally in void-black space
And rain their poison rays upon the world.
Born in restraining cauls of ebon dust
That prophesy dark doom and damnation,
They tear their way through with hideous teeth—
Dark holes that strip the souls of living suns.
In the freezing silence, the dark stars feed
Upon the earth and every living thing,
Leaving naught but hollow shells that crumble
And scatter in the wind between the stars.

The Star's Prisoner

Through ragged bars, the vile star sings
Its languid song of deathless spheres
While sightlessly I stare,
A beast in chains upon a bed of stone.

In a dank cage, it leaves me cold
To bask in its infernal rays—
Forever to behold
The endless blackness of its darkling soul.

In ghoulish caverns of the night,
It soars above my helplessness
And cruelly drinks my life,
A sacrifice to all its brazen gods.

And how did I become its pawn,
The victim of its monstrous thirst?
I sought for deepest truth
And found instead the death that lies beneath.

The Star's Prisoner

IV. THE STAR'S PRISONER

The Stars Are Black

Above me there is only the indigo sky with its flare of dying twilight bleeding away into the endless vacuum of night. In the spreading darkness beyond the reach of day's lost light, multitudes of kaleidoscopic solar spheres, a myriad of pulsing, ever-changing color grows steadily brighter as the light recedes. I peer sharply into the sparkling dome of the heavens, feeling the weight of my body suddenly slip and then slide away like a billowing shroud, leaving me weightless and adrift in the blackness that reaches for me from above. In the now ebon sky, tendrils of essential night stream down from the spaces between the stars, enveloping and penetrating the wraith I have become. All around me, great arms of black undulate and serpentine like sargasso in a nocturnal sea. A burning cold seeps into my being from the crawling web that surrounds me; and then I am drawn into the starry depths, torn by cosmic forces from the familiar bounds of earthly sanity, and hurled into a realm of utter and eternal darkness. Bereft of light and form, drowning in a claustrophobic terror that teeters on the verge of madness, I drift through viscous blackness for a measureless span until my strained nerves sense that I am approaching things vast and yet unknowable in this sightless space. And there is a sound, faint at first but growing ever louder, as of a great cataract plunging into stygian depths. And then with a stunning suddenness I pierce the veil of uttermost darkness to see that I am surrounded by black orbs shrouded in clouds of ebon dust that swirl and surge in the dark energy that bleeds endlessly from their black surfaces. The sound seems to arise from the constant flow of this force streaming into the void, and I can feel it pushing me like a wind-blown cloud back toward the veil of darkness that seems to feed on this outpouring of nighted energy. I again approach the veil, which seems like a sable curtain studded with glittering jewels, and I pass through it with the hissing sound all around me.

    I come back to myself on the couch in my darkened living room. The sound has followed me from that inexplicable realm, and for a moment I again see those vast sable spheres pouring their blackness into the void. Then all I see is a swarming wall of black-and-white that slowly resolves into the image on my television. I press a button on the remote and the room is plunged into black silence.

At the End of Day

And at the end of day
The failing light leaves black
Holes where the trees once were
Like deep wells to oblivion.

V. The Canker Within

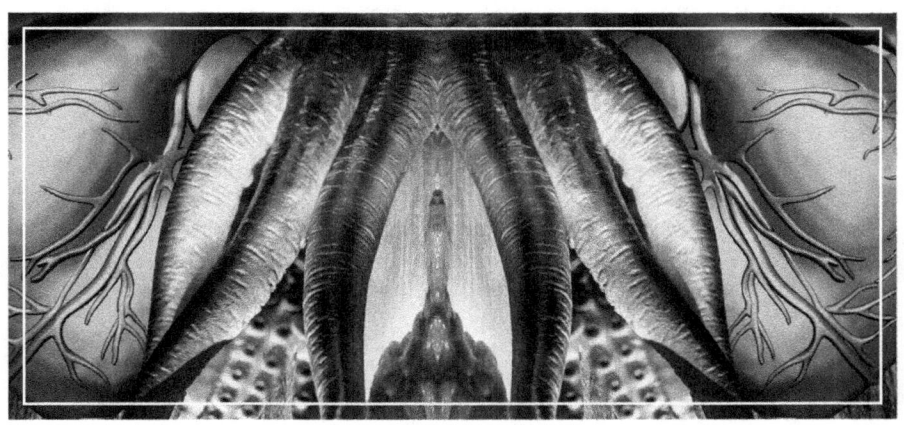

~ Horror ~

The Demon Road

A swirling, slithering impression
Clings to blighted consciousness;
Curves sinuously in ever-increasing waves
Toward a destination smudged and broken.
Eyes rolling to a blood-stained horizon;
Ears straining for the distant wailing;
On a journey ever circling
The stygian well of boundless night:
The demon road.

The Canker Within

Terror is blind because it has no eyes to see . . .
It stirs like sluggish eels within each broken heart
And leaves a stain, a copper-tainted taste,
That lives on eternally like the art
Of lost Atlantean friezes darkly drowned
And the souls of poets lost in purgatory.

Deep within the black, silent chambers of the mind,
It swirls cold and hungry like a dire acid
Whose kiss burns blood-bright through the naked soul.
It is a leprous blot, foul and rancid,
That feasts upon the image of the self,
Leaving torn tatters of what once staunchly stood.

This self-distilled and spreading darkness grows deep
Within the soul like a canker livid, spreading—
Devouring all with its blighted touch,
Leaving naught but void-sered shell descending
Into the vulturous depths of Death Supreme—
A lost fading echo that none shall redeem.

The Canker Within

V. THE CANKER WITHIN

Terror

Terror is blind because it has no eyes to see.
Give me four corners and I'll show you an empty room
Barren and cold
Like the perspiration
Trickling down my neck
Clinging like the iguana's tongue
Cool and black upon your breast
As you lie
Upon the moss
Choked stones.
Floating freely in the cyan pool
Whose liquid pushes at the cleft
In your thighs
Eager to embrace your light.

Jack's a Kidder

V. THE CANKER WITHIN

Jack's a Kidder

For Adam Bolivar

He slashed a smile right through their necks
And carved them all with glee,
A calling card of crimson specks
For all the world to see.

With sanguine jests, he teased the town
That kidder Jack was sly—
A sable-coated evil clown
That wished them all to die.

He hid among the streaming crowd
In sight of one and all,
A phantom in a nighted shroud,
A nightmare come to call.

Then disappeared into the night,
Just like the drowning sun,
He left no trace except for fright
To mark what he had done.

So laughing down the shadowed years,
His shade soars grim, undead.
The apex of our greatest fears,
A smiling ghoul to dread.

VI. The Temple of the River Goddess

～ Femme Fatale ～

Hazel

Reflections sparkle
Moss, willow root,
Sun-dappled leaf litter,
The river in shadow.
Smile glitters—
Sparks alight—
Sails
Into the void
Between my lips and yours.

Haiku Four

Her profile flutters
Among stray strands of brown flax
Tempest waves on silk.

The Temple of the River Goddess

The moss-green waves upon the River's breast
In perfect motion claim the sun's bright glow,
And casts its opalescent, flashing net
O'er bulbous columns staggered in a row.
Where alabaster-jadeite steps arise
From out a sparkling, diamond-crusted flow
And mount to shadowed, verdant depths aglow
With rippling, water-mirrored luminance.
There acolytes in silent step ascend
The stair into the sanctum's inner space,
Where plunging spray-strewn falls crash evermore
To crystalline pools lost in mist like lace.
And from the jewel-like, liquid bowls flow rills
That run in chiseled grooves like burnished wine
And cross the inlaid beryl floor apace
Again to meet the River's joyous arms—
But in the shadowed agate-crusted apse,
Beyond the scintillant, mist-shrouded falls,
A quiet terror holds sibilant court
Amidst bare figures splayed in polished wells—
While night-black priests direct the river's flow
In hungry rush to fill the carven cells,
And with runèd blades of night-black metal
Send forth the souls in crimson-colored swells
Into the maw of she who rules the waves.

Waterfalls

How the sunlight glitters in your hair,
So like red Christmas ribbon against the white kitten's throat,
Falling there in rivulets as you toss your head and smile.
Hand me the waterfalls, for I'm reflected there
And my fingers long for them so
To stroke the strands of fire,
To bask in their glow,
To absorb them for tomorrow.
Let me walk in the waterfalls,
Because the air is dry,
And my cheeks are wet,
And today is passing quickly.
Tomorrow may find the sunlight faded;
The curls lying against your cheek,
And the waterfalls gone.
How red the sunlight glitters from your hair,
So like waterfalls tumbling
Dusk-drenched at your feet.

You Are a Temple in a Moonlit Meadow

A presence in the meadow
Breaking its expanse,
You are a temple of jade,
Smooth, silky, cool,
Reflecting moonlight in angles
Curving arabesques deeply wrought in perspective
Like dense, humid jungle-creepers laced with lilies,
Or the dancing eddy-driven
Shafts of pond-drowned moonbeams
Stirred by an old monk's staff
As he squats reflecting on the auroras in your hair
While you lift your face to the wind.

To L——

Withered pansies on the dry, brown desktop
Were beautiful this morning
And as radiant as the dawn glow
That sparkled in your eyes.
So how can I call them ugly and lifeless tonight
When you still are so beautiful?
Though your eye petals may be drooping,
And your leaves may be tangled,
You look so placid and perfect
Lying curled on the bed,
That I am forced to pause
In the midst of throwing them out
And see that they are still as beautiful as you
And just as tired.

Transcended Vision

You are a profile in the night
Of rolling hills and wooded groves;
The cool illumination of night light
Flowing in silence on your curves,
Fairy lights dancing in the mesh of your hair.
Transformed—
Made new—
Etched upon the softness of my evening
I see you for the first time.

Allegory

Persephone's tears
Fall lightly
Sure hands
On lyre strings.

Ashiel's Garden

In Ashiel's garden of gloom
There is no dappled sunlight at midday,
And the silence is only cut
By the grim scratching of twisted, barbed vines
That sway and shudder in the wind.

Her lithe form swathed in tattered silk,
She plays the air with graceful sweeps and arcs—
Her hands painting the wind with vile
Images of things foul, fey, and soulless
That the black garden feeds upon.

Her hands still at last, she grasps
The thin, dire skull that lies between her breasts
And surveys the grey, leprous grounds—
The black-twined things that strain in the now slack air
Reaching for her like lost lovers.

The light slowly fades to twilight
And cold stars begin to burn above her.
As the garden sinks into night,
Her eyes flare with starlight
Until her form is lost
And all that remains are the stars.

Ashiel's Garden

Aisha's Revenge

The sky was black and filled with glowing sparks
The day that Aisha met the judge's flames.
A mob of townsfolk jeered and called her names:
"Abhorrent trot!" and "Devil!" their remarks.

The willow twins' implied infernal claws
Were twined with hers amongst the forest green,
But they could not describe what they had seen
Except to speak of "shapes" and "gnashing jaws."

Then from the pyre her voice rang out this curse:
"That you shall all burn for what you have done
And all this wicked place forever shun,
For through my words shall all your fates reverse!"

And as the crowd looked on in disbelief,
She burst into a swarming cloud of ash
That caught amongst the judge's fancy sash,
All whilst the ravens croaked in choking grief.

A year gone by again the sky was black
With boiling clouds that swallowed all the light,
And townsfolk stared and trembled at the sight
Of day so fiercely crushed and driven back.

And then from out those seething clouds, great jets
Of silver fire engulfed those watching eyes
In roaring sheets of flame that drowned their cries
And granted them the fate that hate begets.

VII. O Dark Muse

~ Sorcery and Creativity ~

Kylen-Xyr

for K. A. Opperman

Grim night held silent on the cusp
When Kylen-Xyr walked lone.
Among the crooked streets and dust
Of aM' Unree, the bone.

His emerald cloak sailed on the breeze;
His lore-lined face severe,
Like Death himself alone to freeze
The heart of Zol' Zamir.

Slate-grey cobbles beneath his feet,
A vial within his hand,
Soaring down the benighted street
Along the eerie strand.

The wedding feast was all aflare
When Kylen-Xyr swooped in.
The door guard dropped without a care,
A green dart in his skin.

With silent steps he stalked the maze
Into the very ball,
And mingled in the festive haze
Till tyrant's cup did call.

The ampule's load slipped in the wine,
White light and jet aswirl,
An alchemist's most secret brine,
A last sip for the earl.

Then Kylen-Xyr swept from the fête
And through the manse's rooms,
His golden target left to fate;
The dark plot full in bloom.

The viscid water of the bay
Lay motionless and black,
When he strode past the shattered quay
To call his dory back.

He leapt aboard; the sheets went taut.
The wind tranced by his hands.
By cryptic philtre he had wrought
From queer and crimson sands.

So Kylen-Xyr left aM' Unree,
His dark, dire task dispatched,
And sailed the black and mystic sea
Toward intrigues yet to hatch.

The Sorcerous Scribe

for K. A. Opperman

Upon his naked bed of stone
The darkling scribe, with furrowed brow,
Dreams of vistas silent, lone,
And drownèd shores Atlantean.

In crooked garret darkly cast,
Of ragged boulders stacked askew,
He conjures rhymes and verses vast
To crystallize the Muse's song.

The winds that whistle through the stones
To him speak words of burning cold,
Whilst terrors from black inner zones
Course from his stylus grimly clasped.

Each cryptic motion of his hand
Magics mad beauty into life,
As phantoms from a jeweled land
Of faery and empyrean spheres.

So hail, fey scribe! Fill our skulls
With opalescent vistas past;
The crimson wine that smites and lulls
And hands us all oblivion.

The Crimson Kist

for K. A. Opperman

In dark and distant ages past,
When blood-red oceans crashed upon
Grim, onyx spires before the dawn
And strange wrack that the breakers cast,

Above the ebon-pebbled shore,
A kist lay glinting crimson-bright
Aflame with rising ruby light,
A thing of otherworldly lore.

Inside its sparkling carmine womb,
A crimson tome of mystic runes
That speak of dread and sanguine moons
Aspin within the blackest tomb.

Word Painting

Your words,
Dry brush strokes
On the moist fog canvas,
Scrub abstractions against my ears,
Place lines of gesture in perspective.
Your breath,
A baroque of filigrees,
Paints subtle films
Along clean moonlit beaches
Where the stars lie in chiaroscuro
Beneath the clam shells,
While the hot-red-center of your meaning
Slips a cool caress
On my burnished cheek.

O Dark Muse

O Dark Muse, thy wine is bitter;
The wild wind screams in the branches hither.
Thy black words beckon with a soulless titter
That swaths my soul in blackest grey.

O speak to me thy corpse-flower sonnets;
Place upon my breast thy verdigrised lockets.
All upas filled by ancient prophets
That whisper sweet terrors vast and fey.

O bring the braided night snake's malice
To fill my mind like a crystal chalice,
In the torch-lit halls of the caliph's palace
Where I am chained in dungeon taut.

O seed my mind with subtle potions
That guide my hand through dark emotions
Across the wide and boundless oceans
Of indistinct and eldritch thought.

O pale spirit, thy black fount gushes.
I follow it as it roars and rushes
Down ivied paths sublime and luscious,
Till from my pen rage symbols dire.

O Dark Muse, refuse no further
My haunted plea through the cold, dark aether.
O burn my soul with your demon zither
And bring to me that which I desire.

O Dark Muse

Poetry Is Sorcery

Like autumn leaves afloat upon
A leaping fire's breath,
The poet's verse spins silently
A sorcery of death.

From vials of orichalcum lost
Red runes does he extract
To snare the soul in ecstasy
And calm the cataract.

For poetry is sorcery,
An alchemy of words
That sears the mind like iron brands
And pierces souls like swords.

VIII. Tributes

With a Love So Vile

By Ashley Dioses

The Oracle treads the land with grace and stealth.
Remnants of mist trail fleetingly away
As, nourishing the nightshade blooms in wealth,
At night he waits for a life to decay.
Few silver strands of wisdom touch his face
As claws of wind wisp by that dare to play.
He is a man above the human race,
Yet his cold heart has found one like the fae.
And with a love so vile, so soon, he savors
Her sweetened torment and her screams like songs.
With matchless beauty, the great Oracle favors
Her pain to joy, until for death she longs.

The Silver Gate

by Adam Bolivar

Jack entered into Faerie-Land,
Which hath a silver gate;
He opened it with trembling hand,
Uncertain of his fate.

The Queen of Faerie met him there,
Suffused in silver light;
Beside her was a rampant hare
Who tempted Jack to flight

And led him to a secret pool,
With waters weird and black;
Who drank of them would be a fool,
But such a fool was Jack.

He sipped a potion poisoned by
A gnarled tree's eldritch sap,
And in a trance he could descry
The cosmos like a map.

Jack saw a sphere of dullest lead,
Where Saturn held his court;
He swallowed infants, it is said,
A most phlegmatic sort.

The sphere of Jupiter appeared,
Great Emperor of all,
By gods and men obeyed and feared
Since bringing Saturn's fall.

The sphere of Sol arose at dawn,
A chariot of gold,
Which westward set and then was gone,
A wonder to behold.

The sphere of Luna cast a glow,
And silver was her light,
Illumining the land below,
The mistress of the night.

Bright Venus winked; her sphere was green,
This maiden on a shell;
Of ardent lovers she was queen,
The evening star who fell.

The sphere of Mars was bloody red,
A cause of endless pain,
Of clashing swords and wrathful dead,
Which placed on Hell a strain.

And Mercury, the final sphere,
Ruled thieves with wit and speed;
To Jack it now became quite clear
What fate for him decreed.

The silver gate yawned opened wide,
And Jack became the key;
Into the gate he slipped inside,
A dark and nameless sea.

And then Jack found himself reborn,
A golden beamish child;
Just as the sun rose in the morn,
His fate was reconciled.

The Dark Road to Harrow

by K. A. Opperman

For D. L. Myers

There is a road that from Yorehaven leads—
A cave of leaves and branches closely wove,
Which arch above a path where phantoms rove
Throughout autumnal dusk, which sorrow breeds.
And as the blood-black leaves go blowing down
That shadowed way, 'mid mushrooms, moss, and weeds,
A wind of dream borne from some goblin grove
Compels me forward, farther from the town. . . .

They say it leads to Harrow by the sea,
Beyond whose rotting wharves all dreams must drown.
I feel a dead, gray fog entomb my thoughts,
I hear the black waves vaguely call to me. . . .
Now I go forth into these haunted grots
To seek that town where night reigns endlessly,
To sail that wide, dark sea where starlight rots.

—After "Harrow" and "The Dark Road from Yorehaven"

Black Oracles

by K. A. Opperman

For D. L. Myers, In Poetic Brotherhood

Tell us the darkest secrets from your soul—
Black oracles that bubble from the well
Where foetid toadstools, with their roots in hell,
Take on the forms of goblin, gnome, and troll.

Tell us the whispers from the space between
Primeval trees where darkness ever lurks—
Where hooded Druids brave the moss-veiled murks
To hold their torch-lit rites on Halloween.

Reveal to us what venom evil flowers
Weep on the epitaphs of poets lost
To time and name, to melt the words embossed
Upon their tombs through slow, resistless hours.

Reveal to us the visions evermore
Nigh overflowing from your haunted heart,
And with the savage charging of the hart,
Lead us beyond the faerie-lighted tor.

Black Oracles

www.ingramcontent.com/pod-product-compliance
Lightning Source LLC
Chambersburg PA
CBHW071127090426
42736CB00012B/2044